This Book

My Loving Family

1

Table of contents

Why live off grid?

Here are 10 reasons people are attracted to off-grid living:

1. Self-Sufficiency: The ability to produce your own energy, food, and water allows for complete independence from public utilities and systems.
2. Sustainability: Living off-grid often means using renewable resources like solar power, wind energy, and rainwater collection, which reduce environmental impact.
3. Lower Costs: Although the initial setup can be expensive, ongoing costs such as utility bills are often eliminated or significantly reduced.
4. Minimalism: It encourages a simpler, more intentional lifestyle with less focus on consumerism and more on essential needs.
5. Privacy: Off-grid living often provides physical distance from neighbors and greater privacy, allowing for more solitude.
6. Freedom from Regulations: In some areas, living off-grid allows for fewer government regulations, offering more personal freedom in how one builds and uses their home.
7. Resilience and Preparedness: Many are drawn to the off-grid life as a way to prepare for emergencies, disasters, or societal collapse by creating a self-sustaining lifestyle.
8. Healthier Living: With access to fresh air, natural surroundings, and the opportunity to grow organic food, many people find their physical and mental health improves.
9. Connection to Nature: Living closer to nature allows for a deeper relationship with the land, seasonal rhythms, and wildlife, enhancing the overall quality of life.
10. Community and Skill-Building: Off-grid communities often emphasize collaboration and skill-sharing, teaching valuable skills like carpentry, gardening, and animal husbandry.

These reasons highlight both practical and philosophical appeals of living off the grid.

off grid revolution

Welcome to the off grid revolution!I've been so excited about this. I've been building this and working on this book just for you. Thank you so much for being here. Welcome to the off grid revolution! This is it, we're gonna get exactly into the details of what it takes to live off grid, first understanding the mindset of going from the City Life into off grid life. How to achieve this? You're gonna learn from all of my mistakes.

This is understanding the rat race, right? I went from living, you know, through that nine to five, through the crazy grime of trying to get through this hustle culture and then directly to off grid living. This does not happen overnight, and I'm here to guide you step by step and allow you to learn through me and this community to manifest your dream life.

off grid revolution

Before you buy land, you can learn all these things before you take that leap of faith, you have to start first with the mindset of freeing yourself from that dependency, from the Matrix. Trust me, it wasn't always like this, you know, Whammer as off grid life that you see on social media. I'm not here to sugarcoat this in any way. I'm here to tell you the truth of you know, I remember it was like I went from the grocery store. My background in the food industry, okay, I've worked in restaurants. I've worked in the food industry all over the world, and I've been scouting and living literally out of my van so I don't have to pay rent and saving for years and years just to achieve this lifestyle. Now, a few years have gone by, and I've been making these posts on social media and I had no idea that it was going to be popular. I understand there's a lot of you out there that want to achieve this same lifestyle, and I'm here to break down the steps for you right now.

What to expect from this book:

Thank you again for choosing to take the path towards ultimate freedom ie off grid living.. All right, I'm going to give you a more detailed look into what to expect from this book. We're going to dive deep, first into the food production, What it takes to grow your own food? What kind of water source that you need. What type of building structure are you looking to build? Or if you can't build it yourself, what does it take to join a community or get into an environment where you're supported to actually achieve your dream life? We're going to get into a few tips on how to make money outside of this matrix, outside of this matrix mindset, in that nine to five world, we're going to really dive deep into all the details. Trust me here on the mistakes that I've made, so you don't have to make those mistakes and actually do what you want to do, instead of keeping up with the Joneses all the time, instead of going from this place to that place, from that job to this job, and actually live your dream life. Now I'm not here to sugarcoat this. ITS GOING TO BE HARD WORK. However if you are along for the ride, trust me it's worth it.

BUYING LAND	**SOLAR ENERGY**
BUILDING A TINY HOME	**WATER CATCHMENT**
GROWING FOOD	**SUSTAINABLE LIVING PRACTICES**

How do you live off grid?

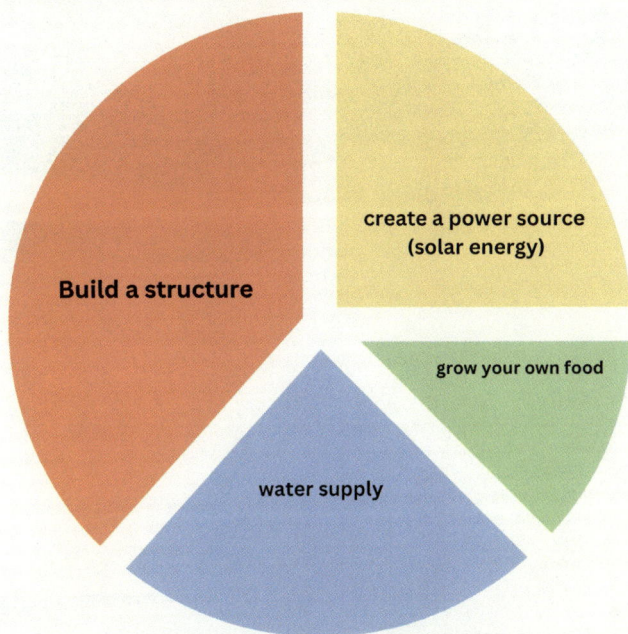

Pie chart segments:
- Build a structure
- create a power source (solar energy)
- grow your own food
- water supply

Chapter 1:
Top 10 Essentials for Moving Off-Grid

Introduction

Moving off-grid is an exciting venture, but it requires careful planning and preparation. Knowing what essentials to prioritize can make the journey smoother and more successful. This chapter lays out the top 10 essentials for living off the grid, covering everything from water and shelter to the skills you'll need to thrive.

1. Land and Shelter

The foundation of your off-grid life begins with choosing the right land and shelter. Look for a plot with access to sunlight, water sources, and natural resources like wood. Consider the climate, soil quality, and potential for food production.

Essentials:

- Land with good sunlight exposure and water access
- Shelter type (cabin, yurt, tiny home, etc.)
- Permits or local building approvals (if needed)

2. Water Supply

Access to clean water is crucial. Many off-gridders rely on wells, streams, or rainwater collection systems. Plan a reliable water storage system and have ways to filter and purify water to ensure safety.

Essentials:

- Freshwater source (well, stream, or rainwater system)
- Water storage tanks
- Water filters and purification systems

3. Energy Source

Generating your own power is a core part of off-grid living. Solar power is popular due to its simplicity and reliability, but other options include wind turbines or micro-hydro systems. A backup generator can also help during extended cloudy periods.

Essentials:

- Solar panels, batteries, and an inverter
- Backup generator or alternative energy sources (e.g., wind or hydro)
- Battery storage for consistent energy supply

4. Food Supply and Storage

Producing and preserving your food is essential for self-sufficiency. A garden is a great start, but fruit trees or small livestock can further enhance your food security. Learning food preservation techniques will allow you to store your harvest for the off-season.

Essentials:

- Gardening tools and seeds
- Fruit trees, perennials, or small livestock (optional)
- Food preservation methods (canning jars, dehydrator, etc.)

5. Waste Management

Handling waste responsibly is vital, especially in remote locations. Composting toilets or septic systems are popular solutions, and a gray water system can allow you to reuse water from sinks and showers.

Essentials:

- Composting toilet or septic system
- Gray water system for recycling water
- Plan for handling waste responsibly (composting, recycling)

6. Heating and Cooling

Depending on your location, heating and cooling may be significant concerns. Wood stoves are common for heating off-grid homes, as they provide warmth and a backup cooking option. Insulating your home well also helps regulate temperature.

Essentials:

- Heating system (wood stove or alternative)
- Access to firewood or fuel sources
- Insulation for temperature control

7. Tools and Equipment

Having the right tools makes all the difference. Basic hand and power tools will allow you to perform routine maintenance and repairs. Gardening tools will be essential if you're growing food, and a well-stocked first aid kit is a must.

Essentials:

- Basic hand tools (hammer, saw, screwdrivers, pliers)
- Power tools for construction or repairs (drill, chainsaw)
- Gardening tools (shovel, hoe, pruners)

8. Communication and Safety

Living off the grid can mean limited access to communication. A cell signal booster or satellite phone can keep you connected in remote areas. Being prepared for emergencies with first aid training and a reliable radio for weather alerts is also critical.

Essentials:

- Cell signal booster or satellite phone for remote areas
- Emergency radio for alerts
- First aid kit and fire extinguisher

9. Transportation and Mobility

Depending on your location, transportation might involve navigating rough terrain or long distances. A reliable vehicle, possibly with off-road capabilities, is essential, along with fuel storage to ensure mobility.

Essentials:

- Reliable vehicle (ideally suited for rough terrain)
- Fuel storage (gasoline, propane)
- Off-road or ATV option for more remote access

10. Personal Skills and Knowledge

Practical skills are a powerful tool in off-grid living. From gardening and basic construction to first aid and emergency preparedness, building your knowledge base will enable you to handle the day-to-day demands of an independent lifestyle.

Essentials:

- Gardening and food preservation knowledge
- Basic carpentry, plumbing, and electrical skills
- Emergency preparedness and first aid training

Conclusion

This list covers the essential components for a successful transition to off-grid living. While every individual's journey will be unique, these essentials provide a reliable foundation. By preparing with these tools, resources, and skills, you'll be ready to start your off-grid adventure with confidence.

living off grid is complete and total freedom

Chapter 2:
The New Era of Off-Grid Living

Introduction: A Shift in Perspective

As the world grapples with environmental challenges, economic instability, and a growing demand for sustainable solutions, off-grid living has evolved from a fringe lifestyle to a practical and empowering choice. No longer limited to remote cabins or survivalist extremes, the new era of off-grid living emphasizes community, technology, and ecological balance. This chapter explores the modern motivations, innovative tools, and supportive communities driving today's off-grid movement.

Section 1: Why Go Off-Grid in the 21st Century?

• Environmental Awareness: With climate change at the forefront, people are increasingly motivated to reduce their carbon footprints and live sustainably. Off-grid living offers an opportunity to actively contribute to conservation efforts.
• Energy Independence: From volatile fuel prices to frequent power outages, dependence on traditional energy sources is increasingly problematic. Going off-grid provides security and independence, allowing people to harness renewable energy sources like solar, wind, and micro-hydro.
• Financial Freedom: Rising living costs and mortgage pressures are leading more people to explore alternative housing options. By building and maintaining their own systems, off-grid enthusiasts find freedom from utility bills, reducing monthly expenses significantly.
• Desire for Simplicity: As technology saturates daily life, many are seeking a simpler existence—one that prioritizes health, well-being, and time in nature.

Section 2: The Role of Technology in Modern Off-Grid Living

• Renewable Energy Advancements: Solar panels are now more efficient and affordable than ever, while battery technology offers reliable energy storage solutions. Innovations in wind and micro-hydro systems allow people to adapt to various climates and terrains.
• Water Management Systems: Off-grid water management has transformed with filtration systems, rainwater catchment, and greywater recycling. These technologies allow for sustainable water use in even the most remote locations.

• Smart Home Integration: Contrary to traditional expectations, off-grid homes can utilize smart technology for convenience and efficiency. Smart thermostats, energy monitors, and automation tools help users optimize energy use, track systems, and identify maintenance needs.

• Efficient Building Techniques: From earthbag homes to tiny houses, the new wave of off-grid builders are embracing designs that maximize space, reduce energy needs, and use sustainable materials. Natural insulation, passive heating, and cooling techniques are being integrated into off-grid homes for increased comfort.

Section 3: Community and Support Networks

• Off-Grid Communities: The isolation traditionally associated with off-grid living is fading as new communities form around shared values. Intentional communities, eco-villages, and co-housing arrangements are offering like-minded individuals the chance to collaborate and support each other.

• Online Knowledge Sharing: With a vast amount of information available online, anyone can learn the essentials of off-grid living. Forums, YouTube channels, and social media groups allow people to share tips, experiences, and solutions.

• Workshops and Skill Sharing: Hands-on workshops in permaculture, natural building, and energy systems are gaining popularity. These events teach practical skills, while also fostering a network of individuals who support and inspire each other.

• Local and Global Movements: The off-grid movement is being embraced worldwide, with governments, non-profits, and social initiatives increasingly supporting sustainable practices. Some places offer tax incentives, grants, and resources for those going off-grid.

Section 4: Redefining Success and Self-Sufficiency

• A New Definition of Wealth: For many, the new era of off-grid living isn't just about survival; it's about thriving. Off-grid individuals often define success by their ability to live in harmony with nature, maintain health, and achieve independence. Success now includes skills in gardening, construction, and energy management.

• Health and Wellness Benefits: Many off-gridders report physical and mental health improvements due to their lifestyle. Living close to nature, growing one's food, and engaging in regular physical labor contribute to overall well-being.

• Resilience and Adaptability: The new off-grid lifestyle prioritizes resilience, teaching skills that help individuals adapt to changing circumstances, from weather events to economic downturns.

Section 5: The Future of Off-Grid Living

• Challenges Ahead: Despite the growth of the movement, challenges remain, including regulatory barriers, access to land, and initial costs. This section addresses these obstacles and discusses solutions, like community land trusts, partnerships, and flexible building permits.
• Emerging Trends: The future of off-grid living may involve more collaborations with cities, as urban areas adopt off-grid techniques for sustainability. Hybrid systems, like community solar projects and shared gardens, could bridge the gap between urban and rural self-sufficiency.
• Inspiring the Next Generation: As interest grows among younger generations, schools, and educational programs are beginning to offer courses on sustainability and self-sufficiency. The off-grid lifestyle will continue to evolve as new minds innovate and adapt the principles for future generations.

Conclusion: Living a Life of Purpose and Freedom

The new era of off-grid living represents more than a lifestyle; it's a mindset shift toward resilience, independence, and a deeper connection with the world. By embracing innovation, community, and a dedication to sustainability, today's off-gridders are paving the way for a more self-sufficient future. Whether you're motivated by environmental concerns, financial independence, or a desire for simplicity, this movement offers a path to a life that is as fulfilling as it is free.

How much does off grid life cost?

You don't need a million dollars. You don't need this huge budget. I started with zero money, zero skills, just talking to my neighbors learning what it takes getting into this. I went from living in my van, raising a family, doing all the juggling all at once, okay? And if I can do it, I know you can. Realistically expect to spend $10-50k for land, another $20k for your tiny home and $1-5k on your own electricity source (solar) and the last is water catchment like a well or building a rain catchment system will cost $$ don't forget more for fruit trees, animals etc.

All right, so this is also a lifestyle remember, we are building a community in yoga we call this the satsang: That means like minded individuals, people like yourself, who are ready to break free from The Matrix, who are ready to achieve their dream life. And once you surround yourself with those people, and have this source, through this satsang you can achieve it even faster. So please utilize this book, reach out, ask questions, okay, because I'm going to cover everything. So again, welcome to this beautiful way of life. I'm so excited to know more people like you are getting back in nature and taking back their freedom!

freedom = priceless

Chapter 3: The Power of Mindset

Welcome to this crucial part of your journey. Before we dive into the specifics of food, water, and building a structure for off-grid living, we need to address the foundation of everything: mindset. It all starts here.

Many of you might be thinking, I don't have the money, or I don't know how to do this, or I'm not skilled enough. These limiting beliefs are the first thing you need to eliminate. If you truly believe you can achieve this lifestyle, then you can. Start there. The law of attraction isn't just some New Age or "woo-woo" concept—it's a practical tool you can use to shape your reality.

We all know the feeling of being trapped in the rat race—paying rent, working a mundane job, feeling like you're stuck in a cycle. You show up to work knowing you're just there to pay bills, not living the life you want. So, why continue going through the motions? The way to break free is to first believe it's possible.

Your higher self is guiding you through this journey. The human body, the "spirit meat suit," is designed to respond to your subconscious mind, which is incredibly powerful. When you start using affirmations and tell yourself I can do it, things begin to shift. Remember, you are the product of the three people you spend the most time with. If you're surrounded by coworkers, friends, or even family members who ridicule you for wanting to live an alternative lifestyle, that's their programming talking, not yours. And that's okay.

You may need to break away from certain friend circles or even relocate to a completely different country to achieve this lifestyle. But don't be afraid. Let love and your spirit guide you because this journey toward ultimate freedom is worth it.

In this course, the first step is understanding the mindset you need. Before jumping into logistics, you must align your thoughts and energy with your goals. Start by practicing gratitude. Pay attention to the things in your energy field—the people you interact with, the food you eat, the water you drink, and the environment you live in. All of this matters.

Be mindful, think clearly, and develop the proper mindset to achieve your heart's greatest desires. This is the prerequisite for off-grid living. Let's begin there.

DO YOU KNOW YOUR ZONE?

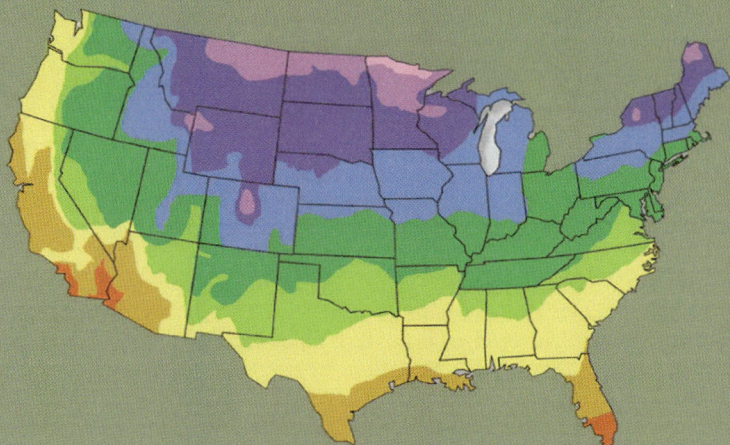

2	-50° to -40°F	**6**	-10° to 0°F
3	-40° to -30°F	**7**	0° to 10°F
4	-30° to -20°F	**8**	10° to 20°F
5	-20° to -10°F	**9**	20° to 30°F
		10	30° to 40°F

Chapter 4:
Understanding the lifestyle

Welcome to this chapter, and thank you for being here once again. Let's start by breaking down what the "rat race" really is and how to understand it before we can create a solution. The world we live in isn't set up for your success—the processed food, GMOs, toxic air, and fluoride-laced water all exist to prevent you from achieving your dream life. You must break free from these environmental influences and start thinking clearly before you can truly escape the Matrix.

This is a proven truth: you can't thrive while going against the grain. Trust me, I know from experience. If you're in an environment where you're competing with colleagues and chasing promotions, talking about off-grid living is pointless—it doesn't align with that reality. It's not you that's the problem; it's the environment, which is a carefully constructed system—the rat race, the Matrix—designed to control and manipulate your mind. This system has nothing to do with the true spirit that lives within you.

Out here in nature, surrounded by the sounds of birds and insects, I experience the raw, uncensored version of reality. You have to free yourself from the artificial water, GMO foods, and toxic environment. You must clean up your diet and recognize that these are all parts of the problem. Think deeply about how you were brought up in this system, which was created to enslave us, lowering our vibrations and keeping us controlled and in fear.

Breaking free from this industrial Matrix or "Babylon"—the concrete jungle, the city—requires freeing your mind. As Bob Marley and other great thinkers have said, freedom starts in your mind. Once you achieve this mental liberation, you can begin to focus on the logistics of off-grid living: growing food, accessing clean water, building a home, and generating electricity.

Remember, you're now part of this community, and together, we can support each other. Let's move forward into the next steps of your journey.

Chapter 5:
Escaping the Rat Race

Now that we've identified the problem, let's dive deeper into what it takes to break free from the rat race and the Matrix. This isn't something personal—it's something that's happened to all of us, and we must free ourselves from it. Trust me, I'm not a trust-fund kid. I lived in a van, worked trades, and traveled the world with the sole purpose of finding a path to guide others toward this lifestyle. It's not easy, but it's achievable without needing a million-dollar check or a silver platter. You can create your dream life for a fraction of the cost.

Step one: mindset. Stop letting the rat race overwhelm you. Instead of competing with others for material things—new cars, new phones—start simplifying your life. Let me share my experience: I bought a van and lived in it for five years, even before I bought land. This allowed me to travel the U.S., from Wyoming to Alaska, exploring costs and potential living locations. I spent three years in Alaska, five hours from a grocery store, completely isolated. I thought this was true off-grid living, but soon realized I needed a warmer climate to grow food year-round.

We all have different needs, so be real with yourself. Grab a notepad and write down your priorities. What do you want to achieve? What does your ideal lifestyle look like? What do you need to eliminate first to start living off-grid? When we get further into the details of food, water, and electricity, you'll need a specific plan, but for now, set a broad expectation for yourself.

Remember, this is a lifestyle—it's not something you just do once. You won't quit your job and suddenly have everything fall into place. It requires baby steps, slowly investing in yourself and learning what it takes to grow food and become self-sufficient. Start small. You don't need a large garden or a greenhouse right away; a tiny tray in your windowsill with a few plants is enough to begin. This lifestyle is within reach, and you don't need a large upfront payment, a loan, or to sell all your possessions to achieve it. Let's explore this more in the next chapter.

Chapter 6: Taking Action – Growing Your Own Food

This chapter is where we get into the real action—what it takes and how you can start now to achieve off-grid living. Let's begin with the most essential part: food. If you can't eat, you can't live. Every off-grid home has some kind of garden, whether it's a small raised bed in an urban setting or a large greenhouse filled with fruit trees. Whether you're on a vast plot of land with sheep and orchards or living in a small apartment, growing your own food is key.

You don't need a huge plot to start. Even when I lived in a van, I grew wheatgrass trays and juiced them manually. It's all about understanding nature's rhythms and what it takes to grow your own food. One crucial tool is the zone map, which helps determine the climate of the area where you're considering buying land. If you're in the tropics, you can grow food year-round, but if you're in a colder climate, you'll need to focus on summer growing seasons and preserve your harvest using methods like canning or fermentation.

Building relationships with local farmers and markets is another great way to align with off-grid living. Supporting local communities brings you closer to the food source and reduces reliance on grocery stores. Even if you don't have land yet, you can start by sprouting seeds—something as simple as soaking garbanzo beans in water and letting them sprout can teach you valuable lessons about nature's processes.

Growing your own food is about much more than just survival; it's about understanding natural laws and how our bodies are meant to live. When I was 18, I started growing a garden in my parents' backyard. They thought I was crazy for doing this when we could just go to the grocery store, but I was curious about nutrition and how we can achieve vitality by growing our own food. Little did I know that one day I'd be living off-grid, but those were the skills I needed to build a thriving homestead.

Whether you're in a high zone like the tropics, where fruit trees and permaculture designs are popular, or you prefer growing in a greenhouse, it's all possible. I built my own greenhouse, allowing me to grow herbs, lettuce, spinach, kale, and more while keeping them safe from pests. This gives me higher-value crops with less worry.

As you budget for off-grid living, prioritize food production. The ability to grow your own food is vital. In the next chapter, we'll discuss the next essential element: water, because, without water, there is no life. Let's dive into that next.

Scouting for the right plot of land is one of the most crucial steps in establishing a successful off-grid lifestyle. The land you choose will determine not only your access to essential resources like water, sunlight, and soil quality, but also the ease with which you can build and maintain your systems. A good plot provides adequate natural resources, such as a reliable water source, ample sunlight for solar power, and fertile soil for growing food. It's also essential to consider the local climate, potential for natural hazards, and the accessibility of nearby communities or services. Thoroughly researching zoning laws, building regulations, and property taxes in the area is equally important to ensure long-term sustainability. Choosing the right land is about more than finding a beautiful spot; it's about securing a foundation that supports self-sufficiency, resilience, and the lifestyle you envision.

Living off-grid and building your own home with minimal permit regulations and low upfront costs requires finding locations with flexible land use policies, affordable land, and a suitable climate. Here are some of the best places globally where such a lifestyle might be feasible:

1. Rural United States
• Alaska: In remote areas of Alaska, there's plenty of open space, and the state offers some of the most lenient building codes in the U.S. However, the harsh climate can be a challenge.
• Arizona: Northern Arizona has many areas where people live off-grid. Land can be affordable, and regulations are relaxed in some counties.
• Maine: Known for its natural beauty and low land prices in rural areas, Maine allows for off-grid living with some relaxed zoning laws, especially in unincorporated townships.
• Tennessee: Some parts of Tennessee, particularly in rural counties, offer land at lower costs and relaxed building codes.

2. Mexico
• Mexico has affordable land and is relatively lax when it comes to building regulations in rural areas. Baja California, for example, is popular with off-grid expats, offering desert landscapes and easy access to the ocean.
• The Yucatán Peninsula also offers low-cost land and a warm climate, although some areas can be quite humid.

3. Canada
• British Columbia and Nova Scotia have areas with low property costs and fewer building regulations. However, Canada can have harsh winters, so insulation and heating are crucial considerations.
• Northern Ontario and rural areas of Quebec are also appealing for off-grid living due to the availability of vast, inexpensive land.

4. Portugal
• Portugal has become a haven for those looking to live off-grid in Europe. The country offers affordable land, especially in rural areas, and a mild climate. Regulations are generally more relaxed compared to other Western European countries, especially in less populated regions like the Alentejo.

5. Spain
• Andalusia and Galicia are two regions where off-grid living is possible due to cheap land prices and relaxed building laws in rural areas. In Galicia, you'll find stone ruins that can be renovated into homes with fewer restrictions.

6. New Zealand

• New Zealand has a history of off-grid living, and certain areas, particularly in the North Island, have affordable land with relaxed building regulations. The mild climate is conducive to off-grid living, though land prices have risen in recent years.

7. South America

• Chile: In the southern regions like Patagonia, land is affordable, and building regulations can be minimal in more remote areas. Chile's stable economy and government make it a popular choice.
• Argentina: Particularly in the rural Patagonia region, off-grid living is common. Land prices are low, and there is plenty of open space.
• Ecuador: Known for its low cost of living, Ecuador offers affordable land in rural areas, where building regulations are more relaxed. Its diverse geography also offers a range of climates, from coastal to highland areas.

8. Eastern Europe

• Bulgaria: In rural Bulgaria, land can be extremely cheap, and building regulations are more flexible than in many Western European countries. The climate is temperate, and it's possible to live off-grid with relatively low costs.
• Romania: The Carpathian Mountains offer plenty of isolated land where people can live off-grid. Costs are low, and building regulations are minimal in rural areas.

9. Australia

• Tasmania: Tasmania is an island state of Australia with rural areas that offer affordable land and a temperate climate, ideal for off-grid living. Building regulations in remote areas can be more lenient.
• The outback areas of mainland Australia also offer large plots of cheap land with few regulations, though the climate can be harsh.

10. Southeast Asia

• Cambodia: Cambodia offers very affordable land, and its government is less strict when it comes to building regulations. The climate is tropical, which is suitable for sustainable, off-grid living, though the infrastructure can be limited.
• Thailand: Rural Thailand offers affordable land, and some areas have minimal building regulations. However, foreigners need to navigate complex property ownership laws.

Considerations

• Permits & Zoning: Even in areas with relaxed regulations, it's essential to check local zoning laws and permits, as these can vary widely even within countries.
• Climate: Ensure that the location you choose has a climate suitable for sustainable living. For example, places with harsh winters or arid deserts may require more upfront costs for shelter and water systems.
• Water & Resources: Access to water is critical for off-grid living, so you'll want to choose an area with a reliable water source, whether it's a well, a river, or sufficient rainfall for water harvesting.
• Community: Some off-grid communities exist where people share resources and knowledge, making it easier to transition into the lifestyle.

If you can dream it you can build it

Chapter 7:
Water – The Essence of Off-Grid Living

Without water, there is no life. In off-grid living, where you are independent of local water supplies and utility services, securing your water sources is crucial. If you live in a tropical region, like I do, rainwater collection can be a great option. I gather over 120 inches of rain each year, which I collect in a water catchment tank. The water is filtered before flowing into my plumbing system for everyday use—clean and free of city-added chemicals like chlorine and fluoride. This natural approach is essential to achieving a truly off-grid life.

There are three main water sources for off-grid living. The first, and most sustainable, is rainwater catchment. With a rain collector, you can capture the water nature provides for free. The second option is a well. While a well is reliable, digging one requires equipment and expenses, often needing professional help for the infrastructure and plumbing, which may also require more electricity. Still, if you're in a region with low rainfall, a well can provide water for decades. The final option is to have water trucked in. Though reliable in emergencies, it's the most costly and depends on an external source, which goes against the principles of self-sustainability and reliance on nature.

Water filtration is also vital. For example, my rainwater passes through a multi-stage filtration system. First, a carbon filter removes sediment. Then, reverse osmosis improves the water's structure for enhanced hydration, and finally, a UV light filter eliminates any pathogens or bacteria. These steps ensure the water is pure and safe, even if collected far from pollution and urban areas.

In off-grid living, sustainability means working with nature, not depending on outside sources. When scouting land, consider rainfall—places with at least 20-30 inches per year are ideal for self-sufficiency and crop growth. Off-grid life is about independence and harmony with nature. With food and water covered, let's move on to the final essential element: shelter.

Chapter 8
Building Your Off-Grid Shelter

Now that you've figured out what type of living space you want and have started to understand what it takes to grow food and secure water, it's time to discuss shelter. Tiny homes have become a popular option for self-reliance and simple living. You don't need a large, expensive house; building a smaller home encourages a lifestyle more connected to nature, where you spend more time outside and live in tune with the natural rhythms around you.

There are various approaches to constructing your off-grid shelter. You can explore natural building techniques, like adobe or straw bale houses, or consider using locally sourced materials. Even without previous building experience, you can create a functional, beautiful home. Treated lumber and metal roofing are durable materials that will help your home withstand natural elements. If you have the budget, you could hire a contractor to help with the design and construction, which ensures everything is permitted and approved.

Tiny homes also come in manufactured kits, which arrive at your location ready to assemble. Although these kits can be more expensive, they're convenient for those who want a straightforward setup. Another option is to purchase a pre-built tiny home, often mounted on a trailer. This mobility can bypass certain zoning restrictions and allow you to set up near an existing home or on new land without extensive permitting.

Off-grid living often requires you to be versatile—you might find yourself acting as the plumber, electrician, and carpenter all in one. However, there are community options if you're unable to do everything yourself. Programs like Worldwide Opportunities on Organic Farms (WWOOF) let you exchange labor for housing, providing access to tiny homes or other infrastructure in exchange for work.

Ultimately, the goal is to create a shelter that fits your budget, skills, and needs. You don't have to be out in the jungle doing everything yourself; there are flexible paths to off-grid living. This journey is all about finding the right balance for you.

Building your own house from the ground up is vastly different from buying a pre-built home, especially when it comes to off-grid living. When you build your own house, you have complete control over its design, materials, and functionality, allowing you to customize every detail to fit an off-grid lifestyle. This process fosters a deeper connection to your home, as each wall and structure reflects your personal effort and vision. Unlike buying, where the layout and systems are predetermined, building lets you tailor the house to maximize natural resources like sunlight, water catchment, and energy efficiency. Although building can be more challenging and time-consuming, it often results in a greater sense of accomplishment and aligns more closely with self-sufficiency and sustainability goals. The experience not only teaches valuable skills but also allows you to create a home that truly embodies your values and needs.

Chapter 9:
Financing Your Off-Grid Dream

Let's talk about finances—the number one question I get. Many people assume it costs a fortune to live off-grid, requiring massive upfront payments for land. This couldn't be further from the truth. I'm here to share everything I've learned about financing and how to make off-grid living affordable. There are various options, such as owner financing, traditional loans, or even using land owned by family or friends. Living off-grid doesn't have to break the bank; it's possible to do this without a $50,000 or $100,000 investment.

Take time to explore potential locations. Some of the best off-grid opportunities are in South America, including Costa Rica and Brazil. In the continental U.S., places like Alaska, Montana, and Tennessee are popular choices. In Europe, countries like Portugal have appealing options. Keep in mind, though, that some regions, like Germany, have stricter regulations for off-grid living, so research is crucial.

When looking for land, skip middleman websites. Instead, reach out directly to landowners for the best deals and locations. It took me years to find my ideal spot, and it's essential to connect with a community of like-minded people to share insights. The journey may require travel or even relocating across the country. I had to leave California due to the high costs and regulatory barriers, but that decision made my off-grid dream possible.

Living off-grid is an adventure, and financing it doesn't have to be out of reach. With patience, research, and the right community, you can find a way to make this lifestyle fit your budget.

Make your off-grid dreams a reality

Chapter 10:
Alternative Financing Options

In this chapter, we'll explore the conventional loan method for financing your off-grid property and compare it with owner financing. A traditional loan or mortgage might be an option if you have a decent down payment, a good credit score, and are willing to go through the bank's process. The advantage of a conventional loan is the security and immediate setup it provides. With a bank-financed property, you can focus on your garden, animals, and homesteading without needing to build a house from scratch. However, the downside is the high upfront cost, and if you miss payments, the bank can repossess your investment.

A conventional loan is the fastest way to get started if building isn't for you, but it's also one of the more expensive options. My personal recommendation is owner financing, which I used to secure my property. You can find owner-financed land on platforms like Craigslist and Facebook Marketplace. Seeing the land in person is invaluable. Check the soil, meet the neighbors, and make sure the local community aligns with your lifestyle goals. Finding land with suitable resources and a supportive environment is essential.

Consider these options carefully as you move forward in your off-grid journey. Each financing method has unique pros and cons, so choose the one that best fits your goals and circumstances.

**You can't pick the fruit the same day
you plant the seed**

Chapter 11:
The DIY Method

This chapter covers the complete DIY approach to off-grid living. The DIY method is the grassroots option for building your own house, where you take on every role—plumber, electrician, carpenter, engineer, and even mail and trash services. While it requires significant energy, it allows you to work within a smaller budget. With a DIY mindset, you can save substantially by avoiding contractor fees and expensive engineering plans.

However, it's essential to research building regulations before purchasing land. Some states restrict rainwater catchment, front yard gardens, or even off-grid living itself. Regulations vary, so location is a critical factor in your planning. Use this community for support; members with similar experiences can offer guidance on location, permitting processes, and DIY tips.

The DIY route may be challenging, but it's rewarding. Building your home yourself provides an unparalleled sense of freedom and personal connection to your space. Each nail, window, and planted seed carries memories and adds to a legacy you're creating—not only for yourself but for future generations. This personal freedom and connection to your home are priceless.

Chapter 12:
Setting Up Your Off-Grid Power

Now that you have your food, water, and shelter set up, it's time to address electricity. Off-grid living means finding alternative power sources, and solar energy is often the most efficient and cost-effective choice. While wind or hydro energy are options, solar power is typically the easiest to implement. Look for high-quality solar panels; used panels can be found affordably and still meet your needs. For example, three solar panels may provide enough power for basic appliances and electronics.

Start by calculating your wattage needs. Check the wattage labels on your essential appliances to ensure your system can handle them. A basic solar power setup includes solar panels, a solar charge controller (preferably an MPPT controller for higher efficiency), a battery bank, and a solar inverter to convert DC to AC power. Lithium batteries are highly recommended for their durability and efficiency, allowing nearly full depletion without damage, unlike traditional lead-acid batteries.

An initial investment in quality components will pay off long-term. Solar systems can be purchased as complete kits or built piece by piece according to your budget. Upcycling used components is another great way to save money. Also, consider your home's power demands, especially high-energy items like refrigerators. With a well-planned setup, you can enjoy modern conveniences, even Netflix, while living off-grid. Prioritize high-quality components, invest in reliable batteries, and scale your system as needed. With the right planning and budgeting, you'll achieve a sustainable and effective power setup for your off-grid home.

Harnessing the power of the sun

Chapter 13:
Things I wish I would have
known before moving off grid

As I reflect on my journey, there are things I wish I had done sooner to ease my off-grid transition. Organic gardening, especially with raised beds, greenhouses, and permaculture, is essential to creating a sustainable food source. One key lesson I learned is the value of prioritizing the garden and fruit trees over the shelter itself. Fruit trees can take 5, 10, or even 15 years to bear fruit, so planting them as soon as possible is crucial, whether on raw land or an existing property.

If I could start over, I'd plant a dozen fruit trees on day one, gradually creating an orchard with permaculture techniques, raised beds, and a greenhouse. The sooner you establish a self-sustaining garden, the faster you can reduce trips to farmers' markets and grocery stores, giving you more time to enjoy nature and connect with your community. Budgeting for your garden and fruit trees is as important as budgeting for your shelter, as a thriving garden will provide long-term sustainability for you and your family.

Connecting with the local community is another vital step. Talk to your neighbors and tap into their knowledge; they are a valuable resource. Before buying land, visit the area, meet the locals, and ensure their practices align with your goals. Building these relationships early on will support your journey and help you avoid legal or logistical issues.

Growing food is like printing your own money

Chapter 14:
Building Permits and Code Compliance

Introduction

Moving off the grid is an exciting journey, but it's essential to understand the rules and requirements that come with building an off-grid home. In this chapter, we'll explore why building permits and codes matter, even if you're planning to be self-sufficient. While codes and permits might seem like a hassle, they play an essential role in protecting you and your property. Let's walk through what you need to know to stay compliant and avoid unexpected obstacles in your off-grid build

.

1. Understanding Local Regulations
Researching Zoning Laws

Before you start building, take some time to understand the local zoning laws and building regulations. These vary by location and can impact where and how you build your off-grid home. Some areas are more open to off-grid living than others, so be sure to research the area's approach to alternative housing and renewable energy systems. Local municipalities or county offices usually have zoning information, and you can often access it online

.

Permits and Planning Requirements

Building a home requires specific permits to ensure safety and environmental standards are met. Common permits for off-grid homes may include structural, electrical, plumbing, and sometimes renewable energy system permits. Additionally, some locations may require you to submit a site plan detailing where structures, septic systems, and water sources will be placed.

Where to Get Information

If you're unsure where to start, visit your county or city's building and planning office. Many local authorities provide guidance on their websites, and some even offer downloadable forms and step-by-step checklists. Chatting with someone in the planning department can also help you clarify requirements specific to your situation.

2. Navigating Building Permits
Types of Permits You May Need

For an off-grid property, you might need several permits based on your location and plans. Here's a breakdown of common permits:
• Structural Permit: Required for most buildings to ensure the structure's safety.
• Electrical Permit: Needed if you're wiring solar panels, wind turbines, or a backup generator.
• Plumbing Permit: Required for indoor plumbing, especially if you're connecting to a well or a septic system.
• Alternative Systems Permit: Many areas require permits for unique systems, like composting toilets or rainwater catchment.

The Permit Application Process

Applying for permits may feel overwhelming at first, but it's manageable with some planning. Most permit applications require detailed descriptions, diagrams, and sometimes engineering plans. Double-check your documents before submission and be prepared for a review process, which might include questions or requests for more information. Give yourself extra time —permit approvals can take weeks or even months, depending on your location.

Dealing with Rejection and Appeals

If your permit application is denied, don't get discouraged. Ask the reviewing office for specific feedback and see if there's an appeals process you can follow. Sometimes making minor changes to your plans or adding clarifying details can help get your permit approved.

3. Staying Within Code: Key Areas to Consider
Water Systems and Sanitation

Water is a crucial part of off-grid living, so your system needs to meet health and safety codes. If you're planning on a well or a rainwater catchment system, codes may dictate everything from distance requirements to purification systems. Septic systems, composting toilets, and graywater recycling may also need approval to meet sanitation standards.

Energy Compliance

Renewable energy systems like solar panels or wind turbines must often meet specific safety codes. This might include how the system is installed, how energy is stored, and what type of backup generator is used, if any. These codes help prevent electrical hazards and ensure your system is safely integrated into your home.

Structural and Safety Standards

Building codes exist for safety reasons and to ensure your structure can handle local weather conditions. They may include requirements for insulation, fireproofing, or even materials used in construction. Following these codes helps protect your property from hazards like fire, floods, and storms.

Building Materials

If you're interested in using eco-friendly or alternative materials, such as reclaimed wood or earth-based materials, check the codes to ensure these options are acceptable. Some areas may limit the use of certain materials, while others may welcome sustainable building practices.

4. Working with Inspectors
Preparing for Inspections

Once your permits are approved and you begin building, expect to have your work inspected at various stages. Inspections may include checks on structural integrity, electrical wiring, plumbing, and more. Prepare in advance by having all necessary documentation available and ensuring that your construction meets all code requirements.

Building Good Rapport

Building a respectful, cooperative relationship with inspectors can go a long way. Inspectors are there to ensure your project is safe and up to code, and a positive working relationship can make the inspection process smoother. Keep communication open, ask questions if you're unsure about something, and show that you're committed to doing things right.

Addressing Common Inspection Concerns

Inspectors often have specific issues they check for, such as safe wiring, proper drainage, and secure foundations. Research common concerns in your area, and be proactive in addressing them. This can help avoid re-inspections and keep your project on track.

5. Permits for Unique Off-Grid Builds
Alternative Housing (Tiny Homes, Yurts, Cabins)

If you're building a non-traditional home, like a tiny house, yurt, or small cabin, codes may vary significantly. Some areas are more open to alternative structures, while others have strict regulations. Look for areas with flexible codes for alternative housing, and be prepared to explain how your build meets safety standards.

Renewable Energy and Waste Disposal

If you're installing renewable energy systems or unique waste disposal methods like composting toilets, expect additional permits. Local codes may regulate the type, size, and installation methods for these systems. Be prepared to show how your system meets health and safety standards, as well as environmental regulations.

6. Planning for Future Updates and Compliance Checks
Upgrading as Codes Change

Building codes evolve, so it's wise to stay updated on potential changes. Plan for the possibility of upgrading your systems in the future to stay compliant. For example, if your area introduces new requirements for septic systems or renewable energy storage, being proactive can save you time and hassle.

Sustainable Growth

If you plan to expand your off-grid setup, keep code requirements in mind for each step. Gradual, sustainable growth can ensure you remain compliant while building your dream homestead.

Conclusion

While permits and codes may seem like obstacles at first, they're ultimately designed to keep you and your property safe. Building your off-grid home to code can give you peace of mind, knowing that you're setting yourself up for long-term success. Taking the time to understand and navigate these requirements allows you to build an off-grid life that's not only self-sustaining but also compliant, secure, and lasting.

Chapter 15:
Making Money While Living Off the Grid

Introduction

Living off the grid can drastically reduce your expenses, but generating income remains essential for most people. In this chapter, we'll explore different ways to earn money that align with an off-grid lifestyle. These options focus on low-impact, sustainable, and flexible income streams that don't require traditional 9-to-5 jobs. Whether you want to earn a little extra cash or build a full-time income, you'll find opportunities that can work for you.

1. Selling Homegrown and Handmade Products
Gardening and Small-Scale Farming

If you're growing vegetables, fruits, herbs, or even raising livestock, you have a potential income stream. Many off-gridders sell surplus produce at local farmers' markets, through community-supported agriculture (CSA) subscriptions, or online. Products like organic vegetables, heirloom seeds, and fresh herbs are especially popular among buyers looking for high-quality, sustainably-grown food.

Honey, Eggs, and Dairy

If you're keeping bees, chickens, or goats, you can sell honey, eggs, and dairy products. These items have a steady demand and can be sold locally. You might also look into value-added products, such as flavored honey, homemade yogurt, or goat cheese, to increase profitability.

Handmade Crafts and Goods

If you enjoy creating things by hand, you can turn your hobby into a business. Handcrafted items like candles, soaps, textiles, pottery, or woodworking pieces often have a strong appeal, especially when marketed as sustainably made or locally sourced. You can sell your goods online, at local craft fairs, or even through social media platforms.

2. Leveraging Digital Skills and Remote Work
Freelancing and Remote Work

The digital age has made it possible to work from almost anywhere. Skills like writing, graphic design, programming, and digital marketing are in high demand and can often be done with just a laptop and a reliable internet connection. Platforms like Upwork, Fiverr, and Remote.co make it easy to find freelance jobs that fit your skills and schedule.

Creating Online Content

If you enjoy sharing your off-grid journey, you could make money as a content creator. YouTube channels, blogs, and social media accounts focused on off-grid living, sustainability, and DIY projects attract large audiences. Through ad revenue, sponsorships, and product endorsements, content creation can become a profitable business. Many off-grid creators also offer paid memberships or exclusive content to followers.

Online Teaching and Consulting

With unique skills or experiences, you might find opportunities to teach others. Platforms like Skillshare, Udemy, and Teachable allow you to create and sell online courses on topics like homesteading, permaculture, DIY solar systems, or natural health. Alternatively, you can offer one-on-one consultations to help people start their off-grid journey.

3. Hosting Off-Grid Experiences
Eco-Tourism and Homestays

If you have extra space on your property, consider renting it out as an eco-tourism destination. Many people are curious about off-grid living and want to experience it firsthand. You can offer unique accommodations, like a yurt, tiny home, or rustic cabin, through sites like Airbnb or Hipcamp. Offering a guided off-grid experience with tours, workshops, or hands-on activities can also be profitable.

Workshops and Skill-Building Retreats

Host workshops on practical skills like gardening, renewable energy, herbal medicine, or food preservation. People interested in sustainability often value hands-on learning opportunities. You could organize weekend retreats, day-long workshops, or even online sessions for remote participants. Charging for these events can add up to a steady income stream, especially if you build a reputation for valuable, in-depth experiences.

4. Crafting Off-Grid Products and Services
Renewable Energy Consulting and Installation

If you have experience with solar panels, wind turbines, or other renewable energy systems, offer consulting or installation services. Many people want to add renewable energy to their homes, but they may not have the expertise. With the right skills, you can help others transition to renewable energy and earn an income doing it.

Selling Natural or DIY Products

Off-grid living often inspires a natural, DIY approach to everyday products. Consider making and selling homemade soaps, herbal remedies, eco-friendly cleaning supplies, or organic cosmetics. Labeling your products as natural, organic, or eco-friendly appeals to environmentally conscious consumers and sets your products apart.

Upcycling and Reselling

If you're skilled at refurbishing or upcycling, you can make money by giving secondhand items a new life. Find items like furniture, tools, or home goods at yard sales or thrift stores, refurbish them, and sell them at a markup. Online marketplaces, local community boards, or artisan fairs are all good places to sell these one-of-a-kind pieces.

5. Managing Finances While Off-Grid

Reducing Expenses with Sustainable Practices
While this may not directly generate income, reducing expenses

There's nothing better than home grown

Chapter 16:
The Power of Community: Learning and Getting Involved Locally

Introduction

Living off the grid brings with it a sense of independence, but it doesn't mean going it alone. In fact, building relationships within your local community can be one of the most rewarding and practical parts of off-grid living. In this chapter, we'll explore how connecting with the people around you not only supports your self-sufficiency goals but also enriches your life in ways you might not expect.

1. Why Community Matters for Off-Grid Living
Shared Knowledge and Skills

When you're living off the grid, knowledge is one of your most valuable resources. Many people in rural or off-grid communities have been living sustainably for years and have practical skills that can help you thrive. By building relationships, you open up the opportunity to learn from others who are experienced in gardening, animal care, food preservation, and other essential skills.

Resilience Through Mutual Support

In challenging times, such as extreme weather events or supply shortages, having a community around you can provide essential support. Whether it's sharing tools, helping with repairs, or pooling resources, community members can come together to help each other out. Off-grid living is inherently more resilient when you're not isolated, and strong community bonds can help ensure that everyone is well-prepared for any situation.

Emotional and Social Fulfillment

Self-sufficiency can sometimes feel isolating, especially if you've moved to a rural area where you don't know many people. Connecting with your local community provides social fulfillment and a sense of belonging. By becoming part of a network of people who share your values, you're more likely to stay motivated and find joy in your off-grid journey.

2. Ways to Get Involved Locally
Attend Local Events and Gatherings

Start by attending farmers' markets, craft fairs, and community festivals. These events are a great way to meet people and discover local vendors, artisans, and farmers who may be working toward similar goals. Introducing yourself and showing interest in what others are doing helps you establish connections and build friendships.

Join Community Groups and Classes

Many communities have groups focused on sustainability, gardening, homesteading, or renewable energy. Look for local clubs or classes that match your interests. Joining a group or taking a workshop gives you a chance to learn new skills while meeting people who share your lifestyle goals.

Volunteer for Community Projects

Volunteering is a powerful way to immerse yourself in the community. Whether it's helping build a community garden, supporting a local food bank, or joining conservation efforts, volunteering allows you to give back while forming genuine connections. Plus, you'll gain hands-on experience that can be applied to your own off-grid life.

3. Building a Network of Local Resources
Establish Relationships with Local Farmers and Artisans

Building relationships with nearby farmers, artisans, and craftsmen can be incredibly valuable. Not only can you learn from their expertise, but they may also be willing to barter goods and services. For example, a local farmer might trade fresh produce for your homemade goods, or an artisan might be open to swapping skills. These relationships can help you create a local network of resources and skills to draw from.

Connect with Local Suppliers and Service Providers
Finding trusted suppliers for materials like lumber, tools, and seeds is essential when living off the grid. By supporting local suppliers, you're contributing to the local economy while reducing your reliance on big corporations. Additionally, connecting with nearby tradespeople, like mechanics or builders, ensures you have reliable help available for specialized repairs or construction needs.

Learning from Local Experts

Many rural communities are home to people who have lived off the land for generations. Whether they're herbalists, carpenters, or hunters, these individuals often have invaluable knowledge. By building rapport with these experts, you may gain insights into traditional practices, like identifying local plants for medicine or hunting and processing game.

4. Sharing Skills and Knowledge
Hosting or Attending Skill-Sharing Events

Skill-sharing events, workshops, or community classes are a great way to both learn and teach. If you have expertise in a particular area, consider hosting a workshop to share what you know. Not only does this benefit others, but it also establishes you as a contributing member of the community, opening doors to deeper connections and future collaborations.

Participating in Local Markets or Trade Events

If you're producing goods like honey, soap, or crafts, consider setting up a booth at local markets. Participating in markets allows you to exchange goods with others and share ideas. Markets are also excellent networking opportunities where you can learn about other people's approaches to sustainable living.

Collaborating on Community Projects

If there's an opportunity to collaborate on a local initiative—like building a community garden, organizing a recycling drive, or setting up a solar energy cooperative—don't hesitate to get involved. These projects not only benefit the community as a whole but also provide an opportunity to develop new skills and meet people who might become important allies in your off-grid life.

5. The Ripple Effect of Community Engagement
Creating a Culture of Sustainability

When you actively engage in your community, you're helping create a culture of sustainability. By sharing what you're doing, you may inspire others to make more eco-friendly choices or consider alternative energy options. Little by little, your influence can encourage a broader shift toward sustainable practices within your community.

Strengthening Local Resilience

A well-connected community is a resilient one. By building a network of mutual support, you and your neighbors are better prepared to handle challenges, from natural disasters to economic downturns. When each household can rely on others for help or resources, the entire community becomes stronger and more capable of thriving independently.

Fostering a Sense of Belonging

Connecting with your local community reminds you that, even off the grid, you're part of something larger. A sense of belonging enhances your well-being and makes the off-grid experience more fulfilling. Engaging in community allows you to be part of a collective effort toward a better, more sustainable future.

Conclusion

Living off the grid doesn't mean disconnecting from others—in fact, the opposite is true. By getting involved in your local community, you'll find support, knowledge, and friendship that enrich your journey. Building relationships with like-minded individuals, sharing your skills, and learning from others can help you create a sustainable, resilient, and fulfilling life. Embrace the power of community as part of your off-grid revolution, and you'll discover that independence and connection go hand in hand.

Chapter 17: The Unexpected Side of Off-Grid Living: Rewards, Challenges, and Daily Obstacles

Introduction

Living off the grid is a dream for many, but the reality often brings surprises—both rewarding and challenging. In this chapter, we'll look at the unexpected aspects of off-grid life, from simple joys to surprising obstacles. By understanding what to expect, you'll be better prepared to navigate the ups and downs of a self-sufficient lifestyle.

1. Unexpected Rewards
A Newfound Connection to Nature

One of the most powerful rewards of living off the grid is the deep connection to nature that comes with it. Waking up with the sunrise, hearing wildlife nearby, and witnessing the changing seasons firsthand gives you a sense of grounding and purpose. Many people find that this connection renews their sense of appreciation for the environment and encourages them to live more sustainably.

Satisfaction from Self-Sufficiency

There's a unique satisfaction in knowing that you're capable of providing for yourself. Growing your own food, building your own systems, and learning new skills gives a sense of accomplishment that's hard to find elsewhere. Every task you complete, from fixing a solar panel to harvesting your garden, becomes a reminder of your resilience and resourcefulness.

A Slower, More Mindful Lifestyle

Off-grid living requires you to slow down and focus on what truly matters. Without the distractions of city life, many find themselves more mindful and present in their daily routines. Simple activities like cooking, cleaning, and working outdoors become opportunities to connect with your surroundings, which can bring unexpected peace and satisfaction.

Financial Freedom

While setting up an off-grid lifestyle requires initial investments, the long-term financial freedom can be significant. With reduced utility bills, minimized daily expenses, and less reliance on material comforts, many find they can live on less. The freedom from monthly bills and constant expenses provides a peace of mind that's hard to achieve in a traditional setting.

2. Common Challenges
The Demands of Physical Labor

Off-grid living requires a lot of physical work, from building structures to maintaining gardens and hauling water. Many newcomers find the physical demands exhausting at first. Tasks that seem small, like chopping wood for heating or carrying supplies, can add up. Over time, your body may adjust, but it's crucial to prepare mentally and physically for a lifestyle that demands consistent effort.

Weather Dependency

Living off the grid often means working around the weather. Solar power, for instance, is highly dependent on sunny days, and water catchment systems rely on rainfall. Unexpected weather changes, from droughts to heavy storms, can disrupt your systems and routines. Weather fluctuations might limit energy availability or water supply, so flexibility and backup plans become essential.

Isolation and Limited Social Interaction

While the solitude of off-grid life can be refreshing, it can also feel isolating. Limited contact with others may lead to loneliness, especially if you're used to a busy social life. Many off-gridders combat this by building relationships with neighbors or nearby communities, but it's something to be aware of, particularly if you're moving from a densely populated area.

Limited Access to Modern Conveniences

Off-grid life means sacrificing certain modern conveniences, like a steady Wi-Fi connection, quick grocery runs, and instant access to services. This adjustment can be frustrating at first, especially for those accustomed to the ease of city life. While these sacrifices often become easier over time, preparing mentally for limited access can ease the transition.

Self-Reliance in Emergencies

In off-grid living, you're your own first responder. Whether it's a power outage, an injury, or a major equipment breakdown, you're often on your own to resolve emergencies. Having a well-stocked first aid kit, basic tools, and some emergency preparedness knowledge is crucial. Being prepared for potential emergencies is part of the responsibility of self-sufficiency.

3. Daily Obstacles
Maintaining Systems and Infrastructure

Living off-grid often means building and maintaining your own systems for energy, water, and waste. These systems can be complex, and keeping them running smoothly requires regular maintenance. Solar panels need cleaning, batteries need upkeep, and plumbing systems can clog or freeze. Planning for regular maintenance and troubleshooting is an essential part of daily life.

Dealing with Waste and Sanitation

One often-overlooked aspect of off-grid living is managing waste without modern sanitation services. Composting toilets, graywater systems, and waste disposal require planning and upkeep. Learning to handle waste in an eco-friendly way is essential but can take time to adjust to, especially if you're new to alternative sanitation methods.

Food Production and Storage

Growing and preserving food is a big part of off-grid life, but it's also one of the most challenging. Gardens require daily care, and storing food properly to avoid spoilage or pest issues can be tricky. Preserving harvests through canning, drying, or fermenting takes time and knowledge. Planning for year-round food availability is crucial, as is learning to cope with crop failures or pest problems.

Power Limitations and Conservation

When living off the grid, you quickly learn to conserve energy. Off-grid power systems, especially solar, require you to manage your power usage carefully. For example, you may need to limit electricity use on cloudy days, ration power at night, or avoid energy-intensive appliances. Learning to prioritize essential devices and adjust daily routines to match power availability is part of the off-grid learning curve.

4. Adapting to the Unexpected
Learning to Embrace Flexibility

One of the most important qualities for off-grid living is flexibility. Plans change, systems break, and resources fluctuate. Adapting to these shifts without stress or frustration takes time but can make life easier and more enjoyable. Approaching each day with an open mind and willingness to adjust your plans helps you navigate the unexpected.

Growing Through Problem-Solving

The challenges of off-grid life can be seen as opportunities to grow your problem-solving skills. Every challenge—whether it's fixing a broken water pump or figuring out how to store extra food—requires you to think creatively. Over time, this mindset can become one of the most rewarding aspects of off-grid living, as you become more capable, resourceful, and resilient.

Cultivating Patience and Self-Reliance

Living off-grid requires a level of patience and independence that many aren't accustomed to. You can't always have things immediately or easily. Delays in projects, slow progress, and the need to learn as you go are all part of the process. Cultivating patience and embracing self-reliance helps you enjoy the journey, knowing that each skill you develop strengthens your off-grid lifestyle.

5. Embracing the Lifestyle
The Freedom of a Self-Directed Life

The greatest reward of off-grid living is the freedom to shape your own life. You're not bound by utility bills, conventional work schedules, or the constant demands of modern life. Instead, you have the freedom to live at your own pace, make choices that align with your values, and create a life that's uniquely yours.

Building a Deeper Relationship with Your Surroundings

Living off the grid brings you closer to nature, but it also deepens your understanding of the land, resources, and rhythms around you. Over time, you develop an intuitive sense of your environment—the best times to plant, the most effective ways to conserve energy, and the subtle signs of seasonal changes. This connection to your surroundings becomes a source of pride and fulfillment.

Finding Joy in Simplicity

The simple joys of off-grid life often become the most meaningful. Whether it's watching a sunset from your porch, harvesting your first crop, or enjoying a meal you prepared from scratch, the simplicity of off-grid life can be a powerful source of happiness. Living in tune with nature and prioritizing what matters most is often the greatest reward of all.

Conclusion

Off-grid living is full of surprises—some rewarding, some challenging, and some unexpectedly fulfilling. While the journey is not without its obstacles, the rewards are just as profound. Embracing the ups and downs of this lifestyle, from the daily tasks to the major challenges, teaches resilience, resourcefulness, and gratitude. As you continue your off-grid journey, you'll find that the unexpected aspects of this life are often the ones that make it most worthwhile.

Plan 1: Modern Minimalist Studio Layout

Size: 200 sq ft

Style: Modern, open-concept studio

Key Features: Compact kitchen, sleeping loft, multifunctional furniture

Layout Details:

1. Entryway & Living Area:
- Upon entering, a small sitting area with a loveseat or foldable sofa bed.
- Storage underneath the seating area or built-in shelves along the walls.
- Large windows to make the space feel open and bright.

2. Kitchen:
- Compact kitchenette with a small countertop, sink, mini-fridge, and two-burner electric stove.
- Overhead storage cabinets and magnetic strips for utensils.
- Foldable table or pull-out counter that can serve as a dining or work area.

3. Bathroom:
- Situated at the far end of the unit with a sliding barn door.
- Shower, small sink, and composting toilet.
- Additional storage space above or behind the toilet.

4. Loft Sleeping Area:
- Accessible by a ladder or compact staircase with storage built into the steps.
- Sleeping loft above the kitchen, fitting a full or queen-sized mattress.
- Safety railing and windows for ventilation.

Plan 2: Rustic Cabin Layout with Separate Sleeping Area
Size: 200 sq ft
Style: Rustic cabin with distinct spaces for sleeping and living
Key Features: Ground-level sleeping area, wood stove heating, natural materials
Layout Details:

1. Entryway & Living Area:
• Entry into a cozy living space with a small wood-burning stove for heating.
• Two armchairs or a small couch with a coffee table that doubles as storage.
• Exposed wood beams and natural materials for a rustic, warm feel.

2. Kitchen:
• Galley-style kitchen along one wall with a small oven, compact fridge, and sink.
• Open shelving above for storage and a small countertop for meal prep.
• Folding dining table attached to the wall that can be put away when not in use.

3. Bathroom:
•Located next to the kitchen with a pocket door.
• Compact shower, small sink, and composting or RV-style toilet.
• Wall-mounted storage for toiletries and towels.

4. Ground-Level Bedroom:
• Small, separate sleeping nook with a double bed or futon.
Built-in storage drawers under the bed and small bedside shelves.
Sliding door or curtain for privacy, making this suitable for individuals who prefer not to climb into a loft.

Printed in Dunstable, United Kingdom

66834903R00036